Peak District
VILLAGES

Simon Kirwan

CONTENTS

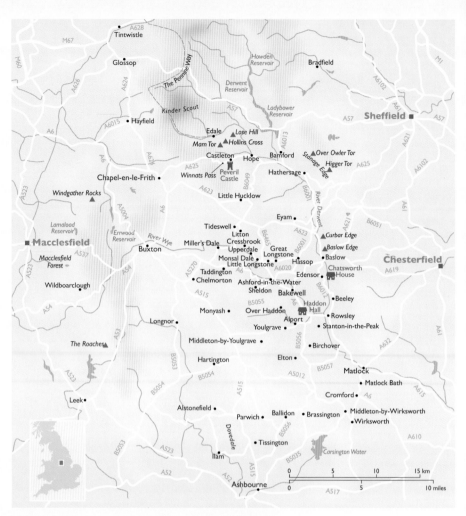

First published in 2009 by
Myriad Books Limited,
35 Bishopsthorpe Road,
London SE26 4PA

Photographs and text
copyright © Simon Kirwan

Simon Kirwan has asserted
his right under the Copyright,
Designs and Patents Act 1998
to be identified as the author
of this work.

ISBN 1 84746 248 0

Artwork and design by
Phillip Appleton

Printed in China

ALPORT

The picturesque hamlet of Alport is situated three miles south of Bakewell, on the eastern edge of the Peak District National Park

Located at a dreamy spot where the Bradford and Lathkill rivers meet, Alport is a typical limestone village. The river Lathkill descends through the village in a series of cascades, which are pictured here. The Bradford disappeared underground for several years in the 1880s, following the path of an underground drainage canal constructed to prevent water flooding the many leadmines in the surrounding area. Although many of the pretty limestone cottages date back to the 17th and 18th centuries, the village can trace its history back even further to the time of a Saxon settlement.

ALSTONEFIELD

Standing high above sea level on a limestone plateau,
Alstonefield is two miles north of Dovedale. It was an important
market town until it was overtaken by nearby Ashbourne

Situated on the beautiful river Dove, Alstonefield contains many interesting old buildings, including an ancient tithe barn, situated behind the 16th-century rectory. The church of St Peter has a doorway and chancel arch which dates back to Norman times; the rest of the church was rebuilt and extended several times in the intervening centuries. Next to the village green, the George is a former coaching inn, and behind it is the site of the once-thriving wool market. Alstonefield is the home of the Hope House Costume Museum, which contains a large collection of outfits dating back to the 18th century.

ASHFORD-IN-THE-WATER

Two miles north-west of Bakewell, just off the busy A6, the idyllic village of Ashford-in-the-Water
sits on the river Wye, crossed by the three arches of medieval Sheepwash Bridge

Most of the beautiful limestone cottages gathered round the church of the Holy Trinity in Ashford date back to the late 18th and early 19th centuries. The abundance of water in the village is the inspiration for the six well-dressings which take place every June and attract thousands of visitors. The custom was revived fairly recently after decades of decline.

Although lead was mined in the area until the late 19th century, Ashford is most famous for the so-called Black Marble, an impure form of limestone which turns black when polished. First quarried in 1748 by Henry Watson, the black marble was loved by the Victorians who used it in fireplaces, vases and jewellery. It was exported all over the world; some fine examples can be seen in the church of the Holy Trinity.

BALLIDON

Located five miles north of Ashbourne in the White Peak, Ballidon is an isolated spot which in 2001 had a population of 79

A lonely hamlet in the Derbyshire Dales, Ballidon was once a thriving medieval settlement but all that remains now are some farms gathered near a large limestone quarry, and a tiny isolated 17th century chapel, Ballidon All Saints, which literally stands in a field.

BEELEY

Six miles north of Matlock, the Chatsworth estate village of Beeley is a small collection of gritstone cottages housing estate workers

In 1747 the Duke of Devonshire purchased Beeley Hill as part of a grand plan to landscape the Chatsworth estate. The village remains much as it was over 200 years ago with houses built of honey-coloured sandstone quarried locally close to Fallinge Edge. Parts of the church of St Anne's date back to the 14th century, and the church retains a Norman doorway, although much of the existing building is the result of Victorian restoration.

BAMFORD

Nestling beneath the cliffs of Bamford Edge, the village of Bamford occupies a delightful position on the banks of the river Derwent close to the dams of the Upper Derwent valley

The 18th century cotton mill closed down in the 1960s and, like many former Peak District mills, now houses modern apartments. The mill wheel survives, and the adjoining mill pool is one of the prettiest spots along the Derwent. The church of St John the Baptist has an interesting design, featuring a very sharp spire and slim tower.

BIRCHOVER

Five miles north-west of Matlock, on a hillside rising to Stanton Moor, stands the village of Birchover, consisting mainly of 17th and 18th century gritstone cottages

Behind the Druid Inn lies Rowtor Rocks, a small gritstone tor, which was said to have been used by Druids to perform magical rites. The Reverend Thomas Eyre carved a cave out of the rocks, complete with steps and seats for himself and his friends to sit and admire the view – now sadly obscured by trees. The Red Lion pub has the unusual distinction of having a 30ft (9m) well in the bar. At the top of the village is a huge stonecutting works and behind are some large quarries where gritstone is still extracted.

BRASSINGTON

At the south-eastern corner of the Peak District, between Wirksworth and Ashbourne, lies the picturesque village of Brassington

Now a quiet place, Brassington was once a thriving centre for the local lead mining industry. The village is situated on a limestone plateau 800ft (240m) above sea level and the area around is marked by the tell-tale hillocks and mounds of hundreds of long-since abandoned mines; in places, there is evidence of old miners' buildings. Most of the village cottages are constructed using local limestone and some date back to the 17th and 18th centuries. One of the oldest, inappropriately named the Tudor House, dates from 1615. Close to the village are the strange rock formations of Rainster Rocks, the site of a Roman settlement, and Hipley Hill. Brassington appears in the Domesday Book as Branzingtune.

CASTLETON

*At the western end of the Hope valley, the picturesque
village of Castleton is surrounded on three sides by the
looming hills of Mam Tor, Hollins Cross and Lose Hill*

One of the most popular destinations in the Peak District, Castleton
has much to offer the visitor: a castle, beautiful walking country and,
close by, the four show caverns of Speedwell, Blue John, Treak Cliff
and Peak Cavern – otherwise known as the Devil's Arse! Peak Cavern
is the source of the small river known as Peakshole Water which
winds its way through the oldest part of the village. Following the
Limestone Way out of Castleton, rugged Cave Dale, pictured above,
climbs to offer spectacular views back to the village and Lose Hill.

Peveril Castle watches over Castleton from its lofty vantage point
above Cave Dale. It was built in Norman times for William Peveril,
the son of William the Conqueror, who the king appointed as royal bailiff
to oversee north-west Derbyshire. Further additions to the castle
were made right up to the 19th century.

Starting in the village is an enjoyable, though strenuous, 6.5 mile
(10km) walk that takes the rambler across the Hope Valley to Lose Hill.
From the summit a paved path leads to Mam Tor, sometimes known
as the 'Shivering Mountain' due to the unstable rocks from which it
is formed.

CHAPEL-EN-LE-FRITH

The name Chapel-en-le-Frith refers to a church built by foresters from the Royal Forest
in 1225, 'frith' being an old Norman French word meaning forest

The busy market town of Chapel-en-le-Frith stands 776ft (237m) above sea level, just off the A6 between Stockport and Buxton. The cobbled marketplace contains stocks dating back to the Cromwellian period and a market cross, pictured here. Pictured below is Church Brow, a very steep cobbled street leading down from Market Street to the High Street, full of quaint stone cottages. As well as the annual well dressing, Chapel holds a Scarecrow Festival, in which weird and wonderful figures appear all over the village to surprise the unwary visitor!

CHELMORTON

Set in the midst of an area of limestone quarrying, Chelmorton is a classic example of a linear Peak District village

Situated four miles south-east of Buxton, Chelmorton is 1,200ft (366m) above sea level and is the highest village in Derbyshire. The steep hill of Chelmorton Low looms above the village, from which a stream flows down, bearing the name of Illy Willy Water.

The church of St John the Baptist is Derbyshire's highest church. It partly dates back to Norman times, although the spire was added to the 13th century tower in the 15th century. Chelmorton retains many medieval strip farms in the fields around the village; some of the 13 surviving strips are visible in the photograph on the left. Many of the farm buildings along the main street are built from local limestone.

CRESSBROOK

Sited amongst magnificent scenery, Cressbrook, once a busy mill village, is now a quiet backwater on the river Wye. It lies close to the river gorge of Water-cum-Jolly and upstream from Monsal Head

The lofty crag of Peter's Stone stands guard over Cressbrook Dale, a beautiful gorge-like limestone dale, north of the village of Cressbrook. Cressbrook Mill, now converted into apartments after becoming derelict, was built in 1815 on the site of the original mill owned by Richard Arkwright. The attractive cottages at the top of the hill were built in the 19th century as a model village to house workers at the mill. Some of the mill-workers were orphaned children who were brought from London by the manager William Newton. Known as the Minstrel of the Peak, Newton had been sacked 25 years earlier by Richard Arkwright.

CROMFORD

Cromford is sometimes called the cradle of the industrial revolution, thanks to the legacy of Richard Arkwright, the famous mill-owner who built the first successful watermill here in 1771. The buildings at Cromford now form part of the Derwent Valley Mills World Heritage Site

Before the arrival of Arkwright, Cromford was a small settlement consisting of a few cottages and a chapel, gathered around a packhorse bridge. After building his cotton mill, Arkwright also built cottages for the workers, a corn mill, the Greyhound Hotel, and established a market. The three-storey houses on North Street are considered among the finest surviving examples of industrial architecture. The large pond behind the Greyhound, with North Street behind, now serves as a duck pond, but originally held water from Bonsal brook to supply a head of water for the mills.

The Cromford canal was built in the 1790s to improve the movement of goods in and out of Cromford and linked with the Erewash canal in Nottingham, eventually reaching the river Trent. Plans to link the canal to the Peak Forest canal at Whaley Bridge were abandoned because of the prohibitive cost of cutting through the Derbyshire hills, and the Cromford and High Peak Railway was built instead. Its track bed now serves as a footpath and bridleway called the High Peak Trail.

Traces of Richard Arkwright's legacy are visible all around the village, and include canal buildings, historic shops (right) and workers' cottages (above). Cromford's mill-workers came from all over the country; he preferred weavers with large families – the women and children labouring in the spinning factory and the men toiling at home, turning the yarn into cloth.

EDALE

The village of Edale is really a collection of five smaller hamlets: Nether Booth, Ollerbooth, Upper Booth, Barber Booth and Grindsbrook Booth of which the village called Edale is part

Edale nestles below the upland moorland plateau of Kinder Scout and marks the beginning of the Pennine Way, Britain's first long-distance footpath which continues for 250 miles (400km) northwards before its finish at Kirk Yetholm on the Scottish border. By tradition, the last stop before embarking on the walk is to call in at the Old Nags Head pub (right), the official starting point.

EDENSOR

The small village of Edensor – pronounced 'Ensor' – is set within the beautiful parkland of the Chatsworth estate; it was relocated by the 4th Duke of Devonshire so that it would not be seen from Chatsworth House

St Peter's Church was designed by the great Victorian church architect Sir George Gilbert Scott and built in 1870 on the site of the previous 14th century church. Joseph Paxton, designer of the Crystal Palace and the head gardener of the 6th Duke of Devonshire, is buried in the churchyard, along with Kathleen Kennedy, married to the 10th Duke's eldest son and sister of President John F Kennedy, who visited the area shortly before his death in 1963. Chatsworth House, originally built by Bess of Hardwick, was used in the 2005 film of the Jane Austen novel *Pride and Prejudice* as the setting for Pemberley, the home of Mr Darcy.

ELTON

Perched on an exposed hillside, Elton stands on the southern edge of the White Peak limestone plateau, overlooking Stanton-in-the-Peak and Youlgrave

The 17th and 18th century sandstone cottages of Elton were once occupied by workers in the nearby leadmines and evidence of mining is still visible in the area. Elton is popular with walkers, who are attracted by the strange collection of rocks known as Robin Hood's Stride, otherwise known as Mock Beggar Hall, and the medieval cave underneath Cratcliffe Rocks. Four large standing stones are all that remain of a much larger stone circle: the remaining stones were pillaged to construct local walls and buildings.

EYAM

Eyam will forever be known as the 'plague village', whose inhabitants bravely isolated themselves in 1665 to prevent the disease from spreading further after many of the villagers became infected

The plague first appeared in Eyam in the house now known as the Plague Cottage, pictured bottom, then occupied by a travelling tailor, who inadvertently introduced the plague to Eyam in a parcel of flea-infested cloth from London. The rector of Eyam, William Mompesson, persuaded most of the inhabitants to stay and seal off the village, even though many died from the disease. The church of St Lawrence contains several

artefacts dating back to the plague, including Mompesson's chair, and the churchyard is the resting place for many of the victims, including Mompesson's wife Catherine. Eyam Hall, pictured above, is a 17th century manor house, built in 1676, and has been the home of the Wright family ever since.

From the rear of the church, a footpath leads to Mompessons Well, a spring covered by a gritstone slab. Food and provisions were put here by people from neighbouring villages, in return for money left by the people of Eyam, who disinfected the coins in vinegar. The plague lasted 16 months in Eyam, and killed at least 260 villagers, about half the population. To prevent the spread of the disease, the church was closed during the outbreak and services were held in Cucklett Delph, a small valley nearby. Commemorative services are still held there annually.

GREAT LONGSTONE

The twin villages of Great and Little Longstone sit beneath Longstone Edge, a high gritstone ridge

Great Longstone is a picturesque limestone village two miles north of Bakewell, sheltering beneath the five-mile Longstone Edge, where the lead was found which brought the village its early prosperity. Flowers now bloom in the trough below the last surviving of the two village water pumps. The water was condemned in 1895 as unfit for human consumption but the well continued to supply the village with water for another seven years. The medieval cross standing on the village green dates back to a time when Great Longstone had a flourishing weaving and shoe-making industry, whose patron saint Crispin is commemorated in the adjacent Crispin Inn.

St Giles Church, hidden away at the end of the village, dates back to the 13th century. Further additions were made in the 14th and 15th centuries, including a fine beamed roof, before a large-scale restoration was carried out in 1872 by the eminent London architect Richard Norman Shaw. This fine church also serves the neighbouring villages of Hassop, Rowland, Wardlow and Little Longstone. Inside there is a memorial to Dr Edward Buxton who, in the early part of the 19th century, tended the village during an outbreak of typhus.

HARTINGTON

One of the most beautiful villages in Derbyshire, historic Hartington on the river Dove is a popular tourist spot in the Peak District

Hartington possesses all the elements necessary for a picturesque village – a marketplace, village green, duck pond, 17th century hall, fine old church, limestone cottages and even a cheese factory! The market charter was granted in 1203, although a market has not been held here for many years. The parish church of St Giles stands above the village and was largely constructed of sandstone during the 14th and 15th centuries. It has a perpendicular west tower with battlements.

North of the village is Long Dale, pictured right, a deserted limestone dale three miles long. Hartington Hall (right), a magnificent 17th century Tudor manor house where Bonnie Prince Charlie once spent a night, is now a youth hostel. Built in 1611 for Thomas Bateman, it remained in the Bateman family for centuries until it was sold to the YHA in 1948. Retaining its country house atmosphere, it is now one of the association's most luxurious properties.

Hartington is justly famous for Nuttall's Creamery, pictured far right, which manufactures one quarter of the world's supply of Stilton cheese, along with the less well-known Buxton Blue. The cheese factory originally opened in 1870 and is now the only survivor of the seven cheese factories originally in the area. The Old Cheese Shop, in the village, sells the classic Blue Stilton as well as regional favourites such as Buxton Blue and Dovedale.

HATHERSAGE

*On the banks of the river Derwent, ten miles west of Sheffield, Hathersage
is a large gritstone village surrounded by wild moorland*

Standing on a crossroads near the border with South Yorkshire, Hathersage is now an attractive village popular with walkers and climbers. But in Victorian times this was a grim mill town, where five chimneys belched out choking black smoke and working conditions were so bad that life expectancy was no greater than 30 years. By the mid 18th century, Hathersage had become famous for its brass buttons and was the centre of the wire, pin, and needle industry, but it declined in the early years of the 20th century when nearby Sheffield developed more advanced machinery.

Hathersage has several interesting historical connections. Charlotte Bronte stayed at the vicarage while writing *Jane Eyre*, whose name she borrowed from the well-known Derbyshire family. In the novel, Hathersage appears as Norton. Hathersage is probably best-known as the supposed last resting place of Little John, Robin Hood's trusted deputy. St Michael's churchyard contains the 10ft long grave. It was dug up in 1784 by James Shuttleworth and a 30in (762mm) thigh bone was uncovered. A bone of this length indicates that its owner was between seven (2.1m) and eight feet (2.4 m) tall.

HAYFIELD

Overlooked by the bulk of Kinder Scout, Hayfield sits on the river Sett in the High Peak, on a Roman road and an old packhorse route between Yorkshire and Cheshire

The 17th century cottages at the heart of Hayfield testify to the age of the village. These three-storey weavers' cottages appeared when Hayfield expanded with the arrival of the cotton and wool-spinning industries. The industry was in decline by the mid 1800s, and now the principal business of Hayfield is dealing with the large numbers of visitors who set off up Kinder Scout, retracing the footsteps of the participants of the 1932 Mass Trespass.

In April of that year hundreds of ramblers set out from Bowden Bridge, where the river Sett meets the Kinder, and challenged the authority of the landowners by walking up onto Kinder Scout. A small group of game-keepers tried in vain to block their route but the marchers continued up to Ashop Head where they held a public meeting before returning to Hayfield. Their triumph was shortlived, however, as a number of policemen awaited their return and arrested five of the party. Several were arrested and some received gaol sentences of 18 months.

HOPE

At the confluence of Peakshole Water and the river Noe, Hope stands in the Hope Valley, below Win Hill and Lose Hill, close to the Roman settlement known as Navio

The stump of the Saxon cross in the churchyard of St Peter is proof of the antiquity of the village, which is recorded in the Domesday Book as one of the earliest centres of Christianity in the area. The church dates back to the 14th century and features the carving of a Celtic face on the side of the tower.

Hope is justly famous for the craftsmanship and ingenuity of its annual well dressings, which take place in July. These beautiful decorations are made by covering large boards with damp clay and then attaching petals, bark and other natural objects to make an attractive picture.

The figure of the climber scaling the west face of Old Hall Cottage represents the Yorkshire mountaineer Alan Hinkes, who in 2005 completed ascents of all 14 of the world's 8,000m peaks, the first Briton to achieve this feat.

LITTON

Tucked away one mile to the east of Tideswell, the charming village of Litton stands 1000ft (305m) above sea level in the heart of the Derbyshire High Peak

The 17th and 18th century stone cottages of Litton are clustered around the village green complete with stocks and an ancient cross. Litton flourished as a centre of stocking-making in the 18th century, and there is also evidence of limestone and leadmining in the surrounding area. The Red Lion pub, 'Free from Brewer', is a popular destination for the many visitors who flock to the village in the summer.

Alongside the river Wye, Litton Mill, built in 1762, is now a derelict ruin, and stands as a monument to the many orphans who toiled in appalling conditions in the past. Many died as a result and the mill is said to be haunted by their ghosts.

Interestingly, the long narrow strips of a medieval field system can still be seen in Litton Dale.

LONGNOR

Situated just over the border in Staffordshire, Longnor lies on the north bank of the river Manifold, close to the river Dove. The television series Peak Practice is filmed here

The cobbled market square and the quaint network of cobbled lanes that wind around the village give Longnor a unique character all of its own. The old Victorian market hall, pictured right, dates from 1873 and displays a list of tariffs for making sales above the entrance; it is now a craft centre. The church of St Bartholomew has roots which go back 800 years, although the present building was constructed in the 18th century. The building is not considered to be very attractive and is best known for the tomb of William Billinge who was born in a cornfield in 1679, lived through the reign of seven monarchs, fought in several wars, and died in Longnor aged 112.

Above: with its quaint cobbled lanes and market square, Longnor is the setting for the television series *Peak Practice*

MONYASH

*Five miles north-west of Bakewell,
Monyash's limestone cottages
cluster around the village green,
near the head of Lathkill Dale*

The beautiful, ancient farming village of Monyash is sited on a bed of impervious clay, which originally held five stretches of water known as 'meres' fed by underground springs. Just one remains, Fere Mere, pictured right, once the source of the village drinking water. As the centre for leadmining in the White Peak, Monyash held a Barmote Court which sat twice a year to settle mining disputes. Monyash became a market town in 1340 and the old market cross still stands on the village green. The adjacent hamlet of Over Haddon leads down to the glorious scenery of Lathkill Dale, which starts at Monyash as a dry riverbed but becomes a river about a mile down the valley where a spring emerges from a cave.

The 12th century church of St Leonard retains some Norman features and contains a chest which dates back to the 13th century.

PARWICH

In a peaceful setting, situated on high hills, Parwich is a very attractive village on the southern fringe of the Peak District National Park in the Derbyshire Dales

The limestone cottages of Parwich are gathered around the village green and duck pond in picturesque fashion, and in summer the pretty gardens are alive with colour. Although quite close to Dovedale in the west, the village benefits from its location off the beaten track, away from the major tourist routes and destinations.

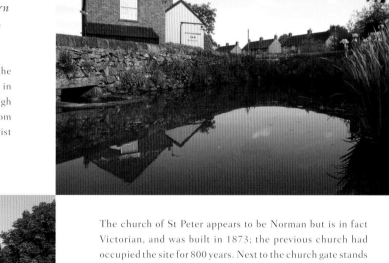

The church of St Peter appears to be Norman but is in fact Victorian, and was built in 1873; the previous church had occupied the site for 800 years. Next to the church gate stands a beautiful limestone Celtic cross which serves as the village war memorial and honours the memory of the men who fought and died in two world wars.

Next to the Dam, once a sheep dip but now home to the village ducks, stands the Sycamore Inn which dates back to the 17th century. Although much of Parwich is not particularly ancient, there is evidence of a Roman field system and manor house, as well as later medieval buildings, which can be viewed as part of a heritage walk.

ROWSLEY

Rowsley is a village of two halves, standing at the confluence of the rivers Wye and Derwent, five miles from Bakewell

Greater Rowsley is the original settlement, positioned at the river junction. Little Rowsley developed as a result of the arrival of the Midland Railway line and the construction of the station, designed by Joseph Paxton in 1849. Disputes with the Dukes of Rutland and Devonshire delayed construction of the railway as the dukes initially refused to allow the line to cross their estates of Haddon and Chatsworth. Eventually, the Duke of Rutland relented, and the line finally reached Manchester in 1867. The arrival of the railway led to the development of a separate railway village, which is now the site of an engineering works.

The Peacock Hotel was built in 1652 by John Stevenson, whose inscription appears above the door. A superb ceramic peacock perches haughtily on the balustrade above the signboard, the emblem of the Manners family, owners of nearby Haddon Hall.

Caudwell's Mill was built in 1874, replacing a previous structure over 400 years old, and is now the last remaining water turbine-powered flour mill in the country. After closing in 1978, an energetic local campaign got it re-opened and it is now open to the public and continues to mill a small amount of flour.

STANTON-IN-THE-PEAK

The village of Stanton-in-the-Peak lies along a steep twisting lane below the mysterious Stanton Moor, where the Nine Ladies Stone Circle and other prehistoric sites can be found

The estate village of Stanton-in-the-Peak was built during the 18th and 19th centuries by the Thornhill family. The initials WPT, which appear above the doorway of the Flying Childers pub, and several cottages, belong to William Paul Thornhill of nearby Stanton Hall. The Flying Childers was a racehorse owned by the Duke of Devonshire in the 1700s. He was never beaten, and his portrait still hangs at Chatsworth Hall, where he retired. Holly House, pictured below, had eight of its 14 windows blocked, to avoid the window tax of 1697.

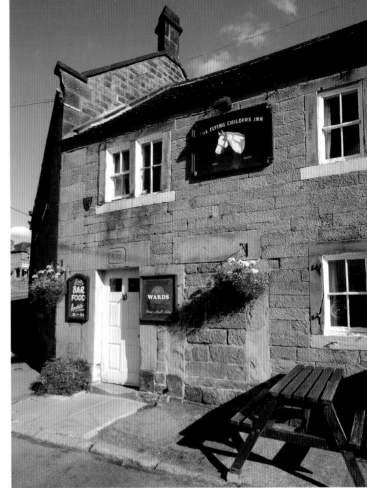

TIDESWELL

*Six miles east of Buxton, Tideswell is
the home of 'the Cathedral of the Peak',
the magnificent 14th century church
of St John the Baptist*

Situated on the river Wye, Tideswell is one of the Peak
District's most ancient settlements. It dates back
to pre-Roman times and was granted its market
charter in 1251. The magnificent church, considered
to be the finest in the Peak District, was completed
in 1400 and replaced a smaller Norman church on
the same site. It was built by Sir John Foljambe, a
member of the well-known Derbyshire landowning
family. Like many other Peak District villages, the
prosperity of Tideswell was first founded on
leadmining. Then, in the 19th century, it became a
centre for the textile industry, producing both cotton
and silk goods.

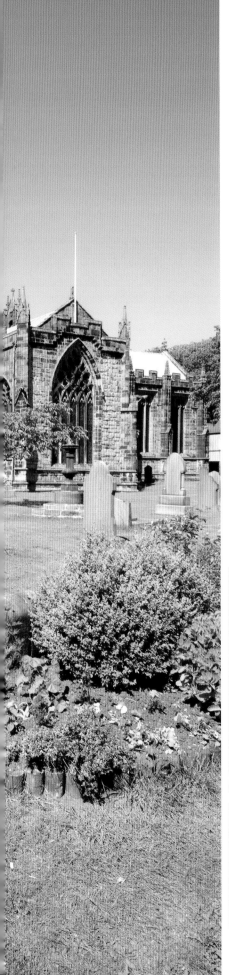

TINTWISTLE

*The Peak District National Park boundary
neatly bisects the small village of
Tintwistle, at the foot of the Longdendale
valley three miles north of Glossop*

Tintwistle and the neighbouring village of Woodhead are surrounded by a series of reservoirs built to supply water to the city of Manchester. In 1848 the Woodhead reservoir was constructed and others quickly followed. The two closest to Tintwistle are Bottoms and Arnfield which is situated to the west of the village. Tintwistle Well Dressing takes place in the last week of June, and in 2005 celebrated the fiftieth anniversary of VE Day.

TISSINGTON

*In the south-east corner of the Derbyshire Dales,
five miles north of Ashbourne, the estate village
of Tissington grew up around Tissington Hall,
home of the FitzHerbert family for over 400 years*

After over 650 years of well-dressing, Tissington claims to be the original home of this unusual festival, although there are various competing claims from other Peak settlements! The village is set back from the main Ashbourne to Buxton road in an idyllic setting dominated by the Jacobean Tissington Hall which was built by Francis FitzHerbert in 1609 and extended several times over the centuries by his descendants. Entered from the main road through a set of fine gates,

Tissington consists of limestone cottages and other buildings, including the Old School House, which is now a kindergarten. The village developed in haphazard fashion, with no overall design and this undoubtedly contributes to its charm. The Old Kitchen Garden still stands behind the duck pond and one of the cottages houses a candle workshop.

The old railway line from Ashbourne to Buxton has been transformed into the 13 mile (21km) long Tissington Trail, popular with walkers and cyclists alike. At Parsley Hay the trail links with the High Peak Trail. Both trails were originally part of the Buxton to Ashbourne railway line which was built in 1899 and operated until 1967.

UPPERDALE

The river Wye winds through Chee Dale and Millers Dale before passing below Upperdale bridge, close to the tiny hamlet of Upperdale and Monsal Head in some of the most superb limestone scenery in the Peak District

The banks of the river Wye at Upperdale are sublimely peaceful. The river is famous for a unique variety of rainbow trout, as well as the more common brown trout, both of which reach impressive proportions thanks to the rich cocktail of nutrients generated by the abundant local limestone. This stretch of the river is owned by the Chatsworth estate, and fly fishing permits can be purchased from the Monsal Dale river-keeper. The bridge provides a useful viewpoint over the river, as wading is not permitted.

The river Wye is one of three Derbyshire rivers that rise on Axe Edge Moor above Buxton; the other two are the Manifold and the Dove. The Wye eventually meets the Derwent at Rowsley, before finally joining the river Trent in Nottinghamshire. The water around Upperdale is generally very clear, since it is filtered through the limestone, although fishermen claim this just makes it easier for the fish to spot them!

YOULGRAVE

On the banks of the river Bradford, shortly before it meets
the river Lathkill, Youlgrave (or Youlgreave, as it is sometimes spelt),
is an ancient village three miles south of Bakewell

Youlgrave, known locally for unknown reasons as 'Pommie', is the largest of three villages – Bradford, Alport and Middleton – which lie close to one another amidst classic limestone countryside. The village is famous for its collection of curious buildings, including the large circular water tank, known as The Fountain, pictured left. It was once used as a storage tank for water pumped from the nearby river Bradford to supply the village.

The 13th century All Saints Church is considered second only in importance to the church of St John the Baptist at Tideswell. Its perpendicular tower can be seen from all over the village. Follow the river Bradford in the direction of Alport and the road from Youlgrave crosses the river Lathkill, pictured above. Narrow Lathkill Dale, with its steep-sided gorge, is one of the most beautiful in the Peaks.